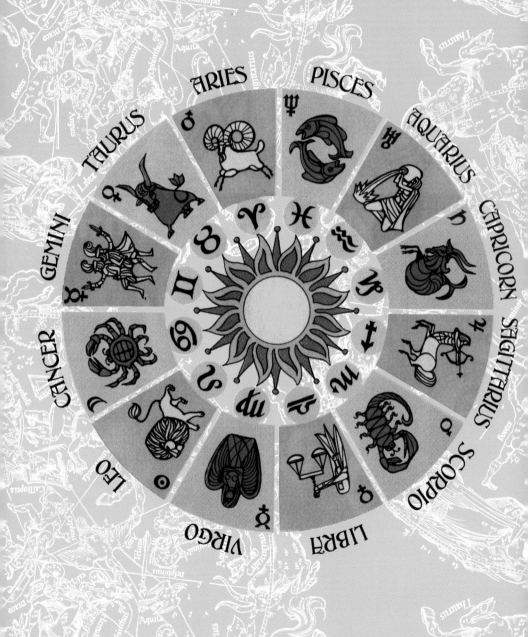

MIXOLOGY

The Happy Hour Astrology Guide

Amanda Beach
Is a professional astrologer & amateur drinker

Benjamin Darling
Has been collecting & studying vintage cocktail books & recipes since the 1970s

Chev Darling
Is a graphic designer & specialist in vintage illustration & design

LAUGHING ELEPHANT   MMXIX

Bartending Tips

The cocktail recipes are in parts (unless mixed directly in the drinking glass) and thus can be adapted to whatever measuring device the mixer prefers, and can be scaled up easily for larger batches. A good standard measure is the 1½ oz. (45 ml) cocktail jigger.

The addition of bitters, sugar, etcetera, are expressed in per cocktail terms and thus can be multiplied for larger batches.

Sugar is expressed in lumps. A lump is a teaspoon. Best practice is to dissolve the sugar in a little bit of the mixer or the spirit or a couple of drops of water. If using simple syrup, a lump or teaspoon is equivalent to 1½ teaspoons of simple syrup. Consider under-sweetening, tasting, and adjusting.

Unless otherwise specified all the cocktails are intended to be shaken or stirred with ice and strained into a cocktail glass.

LAUGHING ELEPHANT
3645 Interlake Ave. North, Seattle, Washington, 98103

ISBN/EAN: 9781514911945

LAUGHINGELEPHANT.com
Reach Amanda Beach at cosmicbeachconsulting.com

Introduction

Hey, did you ever spy a foxy chick or groovy cat from from across the room and wonder what sign they were? Well, if you have (and we all have,) check their drink! Are they holding a margarita? Then you are most likely looking at a cute Cancer. Are they sipping a stinger? That's a sexy Scorpio! Can you dig it? You see, every sign has traits, unique qualities that the person born under that sign shares, even the most out to lunch person knows that! And it's no jive that those traits can be analyzed to figure out what kind of cocktail a particular sign might dig. Like, bold Leo's enjoy strong flavors, so the mint and bourbon in a mint julep is real groovy for them. **Pretty cool, huh?**

Now, all of this right on information isn't going to help you, if the person you are psyched on isn't even holding a drink right? That's where Mixology comes in. With its funky cool set up, you can just boogie on up to someone and say 'what's your sign?' and then spin up their drink using the wheel on the cover of the book, pretty hip stuff. And as if that isn't totally awesome enough, Mixology offers the skinny on the twelve astrological signs and matches each and every one with a classic cocktail, a truly unique pairing, prescribed by the planets and suggested by the stars! And if all of that doesn't get you buzzing, there are recipes for all kinds of cosmic libations, so you can always keep on keeping on, any way you choose. **Most of all, Mixology is meant to amuse you, so... Enjoy! Have fun! And Keep on Truckin'**

Whiskey

Palmistry
The Cosmos in Your Hand

Head Line
Heart Line
Life Line
Fate Line
Marriage Lines

Old Fashioned

- 1 part Whiskey
- 1 lump sugar
- 2 dashes Angostura Bitters

In an old fashioned glass, muddle together sugar and bitters.
Add Whiskey and ice.
Garnish with a maraschino cherry and a slice of orange.

Mint Julep

- 1 part Bourbon
- 2 lumps sugar
- 5 sprigs mint
- 1 dash water
- Crushed ice

In a highball or julep glass crush well four sprigs of mint, sugar and water. Add Bourbon and pack with crushed ice. Garnish with a mint sprig..

Whiskey Sour

- 1 part Bourbon
- Juice of ½ lemon per cocktail
- 1 lump sugar

Shake with ice, strain into a sour or highball glass, over ice if desired. Garnish with a maraschino cherry and an orange or lemon slice.

Whiskey Collins

- 1½ parts Whiskey
- Juice of 1 lemon per cocktail
- 1 lump sugar

Shake, strain over ice into a highball glass. Fill with sparkling water.
Garnish with maraschino cherry.

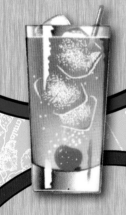

Manhattan

- 2 parts Rye Whiskey
- 1 part Italian Vermouth
- 2 dashes Angostura Bitters

Stir all ingredients with ice and strain into a cocktail glass.
Garnish with a maraschino cherry.

Rob Roy

- 2½ parts Scotch Whiskey
- 1 part Sweet Vermouth
- 1 dash Angostura Bitters

Stir with ice, strain into a cocktail glass. Garnish with maraschino cherry or twist of lemon.

SHOT
Your best whiskey

MIX
Jack & Coke

COCKTAIL
Manhattan

| MARCH 21ST – APRIL 19TH | **Aries** the ram | RULING PLANET MARS |

Aries is the ruler of the first house. The first house sings us songs about self, the start of things, how one sees oneself and one's general take on life. This makes Aries the natural leader of the Zodiac. The gemstone of Aries is the diamond, which makes sense when you realize that the most beautiful things in an Aries life are born under pressure. Ruled by Mars, the god of war and ruler of action, Aries are direct, physical, bold and impulsive. This Cardinal sign means business. *When offering an Aries a drink, remember that they like things strong and fast.*

Energetic Aries can mellow out with a classic drink, like a Manhattan.

Manhattan

- 2 parts Rye Whiskey
- 1 part Italian Vermouth
- 2 dashes Angostura Bitters

Stir all ingredients with ice and strain into a cocktail glass.
Garnish with a maraschino cherry.

BIRTH GEM

The Brilliant Diamond

Tuesday

LUCKY DAY & NUMBER

7 & 8

famous PEOPLE

Elton John
Billie Holiday
Marvin Gaye

Steve McQueen
Diana Ross
William Shatner

SHOT
Good Tequila with an orange wedge

MIX
Vodka, soda, splash of cranberry juice and a lemon

COCKTAIL
Gimlet

APRIL 20TH - MAY 20TH	**Taurus** **the bull**	RULING PLANET VENUS

Taurus is represented by the bull. Ruled by Venus and The Keeper of the second house. The emerald is dear to earthy bulls. Taurus is kind, generous, stubborn, and loves all things that stand the test of time. Luxury, craftsmanship and quality attract a Taurus. As the second house represents all things to do with employment and resources, at times Taurus can be so busy with their work. *It might not attend every social gathering on the calendar, but when you can get the bull from the pen they'll be happy to take nightlife by the horns.*

Strong & practical, a classic Gimlet is terrific for Taurus.

Gimlet

- 2 parts Gin
- 1 part Lime Juice Cordial

Shake with ice, strain into a cocktail glass.

RTH GEM

he Emerald

Friday

LUCKY DAY & NUMBER

1 & 3

famous PEOPLE

James Brown
Ella Fitzgerald
Salvador Dalí

Iggy Pop
Jack Nicholson
Stevie Wonder

7

Vodka

Bloody Mary

- 1 part Vodka
- 3 parts tomato juice
- ½ oz. lemon juice per cocktail
- 2 dashes Worcestershire per cocktail
- 2 dashes Tabasco per cocktail

Shake with ice and strain over ice in a highball glass.
Garnish with a celery stalk, two speared green olives and a lime wedge.

Cosmopolitan

- 1½ parts Citrus Vodka
- ½ part Cointreau
- 1 part cranberry juice
- ½ part fresh lime juice

Shake with ice and strain into a chilled cocktail glass.
Garnish with a lime wedge.

Moscow Mule

- 2 parts Vodka
- 3 parts ginger beer
- 1 part lime juice

Add all ingredients to a copper mug or highball glass, fill with ice. Garnish with a lime wedge.

Vodka & Tonic

- 1½ parts Vodka
- Tonic water

Pour over ice cubes in a highball glass and fill with tonic water. Garnish with slice of lemon or lime.

Vodka Martini

- 3, 4 or 5 parts Vodka
- 1 part Dry Vermouth

Stir well with ice. Strain into cocktail glass. Add an olive or twist of lemon.
(To make it Dirty add a little olive juice)

Screwdriver

- 1 part Vodka
- Orange juice

Pour Vodka in a highball glass over ice cubes. Fill with orange juice. Stir and garnish with an orange slice.

SHOT
Spiced Rum

MIX
Whiskey & Soda with a cherry
on top

COCKTAIL
Kamikaze

♊

| MAY 21ST
- JUNE 21ST | **Gemini**
the twins | RULING PLANET
MERCURY |

The sign of The Twins, Gemini, is mutable and the Gemini-born are highly adaptable. Duality is both a gift and a curse for this sign. They can see both sides but that can often can be mistaken for disloyalty. The third house is all about communication. Those born under this sign are dynamic, chatty and constantly up to something. The natural storyteller of the zodiac will always have an idea to share. *Since Gemini rules siblings and neighbors, here are some drinks to serve while socializing with those close to your own front door.*

The Kamikaze is the perfect cocktail for fun-loving Gemini's.

Kamikaze

- 1 part Vodka
- 1 part Triple Sec
- 1 part lime juice

Shake with ice. Strain into a cocktail glass. Garnish with a lime slice.

RTH GEM

The Lustrous Pearl

Wednesday

LUCKY DAY & NUMBER

3 & 6

famous PEOPLE

Harvey Milk
Paul McCartney
Miles Davis

Gene Wilder
Bob Dylan
Stevie Nicks

SHOT
Irish Whiskey

MIX
Vodka & pineapple juice

COCKTAIL
Classic Margarita

69

JUNE 22ND - JULY 22ND	**Cancer** the crab	RULING PLANET THE MOON

Cancer represents the eternal mother. The ruler of the fourth house, the space the zodiac devotes to home, family and all matters on the domestic front. Cancers are natural nurturing caregivers In fact they are often so preoccupied with taking care of others that they forget to have fun along the way. A sign that is known for it's love for nostalgia, serving up some classic cocktails is the way to this moon child's vintage loving heart.

Sensitive, imaginative and security minded, here are some drinks to help you bring your crabby Cancer out of their shell.

The Classic Margarita appeals to Cancer's nostalgic nature.

Classic Margarita

- 2 parts. Tequila
- 1 part Cointreau
- 1 part lime juice
- Salt

Rub the rim of the glass with the lime slice to make the salt stick to it. Shake the other ingredients, then carefully pour into the glass over ice.

BIRTH GEM

The Ruby

Monday

LUCKY DAY & NUMBER

8 & 3

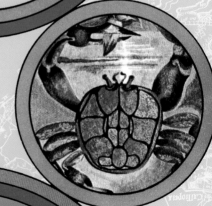

famous PEOPLE

Debbie Harry
Cheech Marin
Linda Ronstadt

Cat Stevens
Richard Simmons
Ringo Starr

Gin

Gin and Tonic

- 1½ parts Gin
- Tonic water

Pour Gin over ice in a highball glass, and fill with tonic water. Garnish with slice of lime.

check your
ruling planet

The sun, moon, and planets each have special spheres of influence. Depending on their relative location in the sky, they affect all people in varying degrees . . . but especially those in the Zodiac signs they dominate or "rule."

Sun : life's central power! Rules individuality, purpose.
Moon : affects emotions, home, and a changeable nature.
Mars : relates to energy, aggression, and initiative.
Mercury : influences intelligence, communications, travel.
Venus : pertains to love, beauty, and the fine arts.
Jupiter : reigns over joviality, wealth and reason.
Saturn : regulates time, cautiousness, and discipline.
Uranus : rules sudden change, inventiveness, originality.
Neptune : governs intuition, ideals and mysticism.
Pluto : newly found planet, said to be ruler of Scorpio by some astrologers ; relates to trends, government, rebirth.

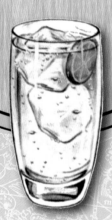

Dry Martini

- 3 parts Gin
- 1 part French Vermouth

Stir with ice, strain into a cocktail glass. Garnish with a green olive or lemon peel.

Orange Blossom

- 1 part Gin
- 1 part orange juice
- Ice

Shake with ice, strain into a cocktail glass.

Negroni

- 1 part Gin
- 1 part Italian Vermouth
- 1 part Campari

Stir with ice, strain into a cocktail glass. Garnish with a lemon peel.

Gimlet

- 2 parts Gin
- 1 part lime juice cordial

Shake with ice, strain into a cocktail glass.

Tom Collins

- 1 part Gin
- Juice of ½ lemon per cocktail
- 2 lumps sugar
- Sparkling water

Serve over ice in highball glass. Fill with sparkling water. Garnish with a maraschino cherry and orange slice.

15

SHOT
Cinnamon Whiskey

MIX
Vodka, soda, splash of cranberry
juice and a lemon

COCKTAIL
Gimlet

JULY 23RD - AUGUST 22ND	**Leo** the lion	RULING PLANET THE SUN

Leo's are known for their royal attitudes and generous nature, a natural leader of the pack. The fifth house proudly tells us about creativity, optimism and a little drama. Leo's are happiest in the limelight and make incredible performers. They are giving, joyus and take pride in their work. When serving the royal Leo, make sure that presentation is everything and the ingredients are sophisticated and refined. *Here are some things to make your lion roar.*

The bold flavors & strong statement of a Mint Julep are perfect for confident, glamorous Leo.

Mint Julep

- 1 part Bourbon
- 2 lumps sugar
- 5 sprigs mint
- 1 dash water
- Crushed ice

In a highball or julep glass, crush well four sprigs of mint, sugar and water. Add Bourbon and pack with crushed ice. Garnish with a mint sprig.

RTH GEM

The Ruby

Sunday

LUCKY DAY & NUMBER

5 & 1

famous PEOPLE

Mick Jagger
Robert Plant
Lynda Carter

Coco Chanel
Andy Warhol
Alex Haley

17

SHOT
Fernet

MIX
Tequila, soda, lime

COCKTAIL
Aperol Spritz

AUGUST 23RD – SEPTEMBER 22ND	**Virgo** *the virgin*	RULING PLANET MERCURY

Those born when the sun is in Virgo are detail oriented, hardworking and devoted (almost to a fault). They may come off as critical, but they really have your best interests at heart. The ruler of the 6th house, which rules daily routines, diet, health and the role one plays in their career, some Virgos tend to internalize their stress, often affecting their digestion. *With that in mind here are some drinks to help them have a good time while going easy on their sensitive disposition.*

18

The Aperol Spritz is a classic cocktail, sure to please Virgo's classic and classy nature.

BIRTH GEM

Heavenly Sapphire

Aperol Spritz

- 4½ parts Brut Prosecco
- 2½ parts Aperol
- 1 oz. club soda

Pour the Prosecco into a collins glass filled with ice. Add the Aperol and a lime or orange slice, top with club soda.

Wednesday

LUCKY DAY & NUMBER

8 & 5

famous PEOPLE

Barry Gibb
Gloria Gaynor
Michael Jackson

Peter Sellers
Jane Curtin
Twiggy

19

Rum

Daiquiri

- 1 part Light Rum
- ½ part fresh lime juice
- ½ lump sugar per cocktail

Shake with ice, strain into a cocktail glass..

Planters Punch

- 1½ parts Rum
- Juice of ½ lime or lemon per cocktail
- 1 part orange juice or pineapple juice, or equal parts both
- 1 lump sugar
- 1 tsp. Grenadine per cocktail

Shake well with ice. Pour into highball glass filled with finely cracked ice. Garnish with fresh fruit.

Cuba Libre

- 1 part Light Rum
- 3 parts cola
- ½ lime per cocktail

Squeeze lime and drop rind into highball glass. Add ice and the ingredients.
Garnish with a lime wedge.

Havana Club Cocktail

- 2 Parts Rum
- 1 part Dry Vermouth

Stir well with Ice. Serve in a cocktail glass with a cherry.

Rum Swizzle

- 3 parts Dark Rum
- 1 lump sugar
- 1 part fresh orange juice
- ½ part fresh lime juice
- 2 dashes Angostura Bitters
- club soda

Shake well with ice. Top with club soda. Garnish with an orange slice and a maraschino cherry.

Mojito

- 2 parts Light Rum
- 4 lime wedges
- 12 Fresh mint leaves
- 2 lumps sugar
- 1 part club soda

Squeeze the lime wedges in the glass. Add sugar. Rub the mint leaves lightly between your palms, rub them on the rim of the glass and drop them in. Half fill the glass with crushed ice, add the light rum & stir. Top with crushed ice, a splash of soda, and a sprig of mint.

SHOT
Just Peachy
1 part Peach Schnapps, 1 part lime juice.
Shake and strain into a shot glass.

MIX
Rum & Coke

COCKTAIL
Tequila Sunrise

SEPTEMBER 23RD – OCTOBER 22ND	**Libra** the scales	RULING PLANET VENUS

Libra, the sign of the scales, is ruled
by the 7th house. Your balancing buddy
will probably want to enjoy these drinks even
more with their friends. Libras are known for
their fondness for style and luxurious fabrics,
along with their charming nature and ability to get
along with just about anyone. Relationships rule
a Libra. From business partners to interpersonal
style, the 7th house talks about all things part-
nership and teaches us about compromise.
*Just like a Libra, these are guaranteed
universal crowd-pleasers.*

The well balanced flavors in this cocktail, make it perfect for equanimous Libra.

Tequila Sunrise

- 1½ parts Tequila
- 3 parts orange juice
- ½ oz. Grenadine syrup per cocktail

Pour the tequila and orange juice into a highball glass over ice. Add the Grenadine, which will sink to the bottom. Do not stir. Garnish with an orange slice and a maraschino cherry.

RTH GEM

he Flashing Opal

Friday

LUCKY DAY & NUMBER

6 & 4

famous PEOPLE

Evel Knievel
Don Cornelius
John Lennon

Olivia Newton-John
Carrie Fisher
Jimmy Carter

SHOT
Vodka

MIX
Vodka & grapefruit juice

COCKTAIL
Stinger

OCTOBER 23RD – NOVEMBER 21ST	# Scorpio ### the scorpion	RULING PLANET MARS

Known for a mysterious nature and loyalty that borders on the obsessive, Scorpio is the ruler of the 8th house. This placement talks to us about the things we have to dig deeper to see. Scorpios are known for their ability to dive deep into the underworld part of life. For the house that rules death, dying and other people's money (such an inheritance), Scorpions can be the life of the party and often drawn to the obscure and curious. *When making a cocktail for this sign make sure it has some sting.*

The aptly named Stinger is the perfect bold cocktail choice for Scorpio.

Deep Glowing Red

Stinger

- 2 parts Brandy
- 1 part Crème de Menthe
- Ice

Stir, strain into a cocktail glass.

BIRTH GEM

The Golden Topaz

Tuesday

LUCKY DAY & NUMBER

5 & 4

famous PEOPLE

Joni Mitchell
Henry Winkler
Art Garfunkel

Grace Slick
Kurt Vonnegut
Mahalia Jackson

Brandy

Brandy Cocktail

- 2 parts Brandy
- ½ part Orange Curacao Liqueur
- 2 dashes Angostura Bitters
- 2 dashes Peychaud's Bitters
    per drink

Shake well with ice. Strain into a
cocktail glass.
Garnish with a lemon peel.

Birth Gems and Colors

that you were born to wear !

 ARIES : gem is the brilliant diamond ;
color is bright, fiery red.

 TAURUS : gem is the emerald. Colors
are Spring's green and yellow.

 GEMINI : gem is the lustrous pearl ;
colors are clear blue and gray.

 CANCER : gems are ruby and moon-
stone ; colors are silver and white.

 LEO : gems are sardonyx and ruby.
Colors are sunny orange and gold.

 VIRGO : gem is the heavenly sapphire. Color is sapphire blue.

 LIBRA : gem is the flashing opal ;
colors are airy blue and gold.

 SCORPIO : gem is the golden topaz.
Color is deep, glowing red.

 SAGITTARIUS : gem is the intriguing
turquoise. Color is royal purple.

 CAPRICORN : gem is the garnet.
Colors are black and rich brown.

 AQUARIUS : gem is the alluring
amethyst. Color is electric blue.

PISCES : gem is the aquamarine.
Colors are sea green and lavender.

Metropolitan

- 1 part Brandy
- 1 part Italian Vermouth
- 1 lump sugar
- 1 dash Angostura Bitters
    per cocktail

Shake well with ice, strain into a
cocktail glass.

Club Cocktail

- 2 parts.Brandy
- ½ part Maraschino Liqueur
- ½ part pineapple juice
- 2 dashes Peychaud's Bitters

Shake all ingredients well with ice and strain into a martini or cocktail glass. Garnish with a twist of lemon peel and a strawberry, and serve.

Vieux Carre

- ¾ part Rye Whiskey
- ¾ part Cognac
- ¾ part Sweet Vermouth
- 2 dashes Peychaud's Bitters per cocktail
- 2 dashes Angostura Bitters
- ½ teaspoon Benedictine Liqueur per cocktail

Stir well with ice. Strain into an old fashioned glass filled with ice. Garnish with a cherry.

Champagne Cocktail

- $^1/_3$ part Cognac
- 3 parts Champagne
- Dash Angostura bitters
- 1 Sugar cube

Add dash of Angostura Bitters onto sugar cube and drop it into champagne flute. Add Cognac followed by gently pouring chilled Champagne. Garnish with orange slice and maraschino cherry.

Sidecar

- 1½ parts Cognac
- 1 part Triple Sec
- ½ part lemon juice

Shake with ice. Strain into a cocktail glass.
Option: sugar, rim of glass.

SHOT
Whatever you're having

MIX
Vodka Soda with an orange

COCKTAIL
Screwdriver

NOVEMBER 22ND - DECEMBER 21ST	**Sagittarius** the archer	RULING PLANET JUPITER

The sign of the Archer is often known for setting it's mind on a target and getting what it wants. When wooing a Sagittarius, it's important to recognize their passion for all things exotic. The ninth house rules foreign people, places and things, along with higher education. Sagittarius are optimistic, freedom loving and enjoy living their best life. Sagittarius love to laugh and enjoy a good night out. Don't worry about being too out there or over the top when serving a Sagittarius.

The sign of expansion and adventure can't wait to drink these while telling you all about their next vacation.

The Screwdriver comes to straight to the point for straight forward Sagittarius.

Screwdriver

- 1 part Vodka
- Orange juice

Pour Vodka in a highball glass over ice cubes. Fill with orange juice. Stir and garnish with an orange slice.

RTH GEM

e Intriguing Turquoise

Thursday

LUCKY DAY & NUMBER

9

famous PEOPLE

Jimi Hendrix
Jane Fonda
Jim Morrison

Richard Pryor
Tina Turner
Billie Jean King

SHOT
Breakfast Shot
¼ parts Butterscotch Schnapps,
¾ parts Irish Whiskey, ½ part O.J.

MIX
7 & 7

COCKTAIL
Gin & Tonic

DECEMBER 22ND –
JANUARY 19TH

Capricorn
the goat

RULING PLANET
SATURN

The sign of the Goat is known for being responsible, disciplined and hardworking. Capricorns aren't afraid to climb high to complete their goals. You'll often find them working late, getting up early and making sure that things are in order. They are loyal, practical and very loving. *When cutting loose, remember to offer your Saturn ruled friend something they can savor.*

The good old G & T will appeal to Capricorn's practical nature.

Gin & Tonic

- 1½ parts Gin
- Tonic water
- Ice

Pour gin over ice in a highball glass, and fill with tonic water.
Garnish with slice of lime

IRTH GEM

he Garnet

Saturday

LUCKY DAY & NUMBER

7 & 8

famous PEOPLE

David Bowie
Elvis Presley
Rod Stewart

Donna Summer
Janis Joplin
Jimmy Page

31

Tequila

Classic Margarita

- 2 parts Tequila
- 1 part Cointreau
- 1 part lime juice
- Salt

Rub the rim of an old fashioned glass with the lime slice to make the salt stick to it. Shake the other ingredients with ice, then carefully pour into the glass.

Tequila Sunrise

- 1½ parts Tequila
- 3 parts orange juice
- ½ oz. Grenadine syrup per cocktail

Pour the Tequila and orange juice into a highball glass over ice. Add the Grenadine, which will sink to the bottom. Do not stir. Garnish with orange slice and a maraschino cherry.

Tequila Sour

- 2 parts Reposado Tequila
- 1 part fresh-squeezed lemon juice
- 1 lump sugar
- Dash of Angostura Orange Bitters per cocktail
- 1 teaspoon egg white (optional)

Shake with ice. Strain into sour or wine glass. Garnish with a lemon slice and a cherry.

Juan Collins

- 1½ parts Tequila
- 1 part lemon juice
- 1 part agave nectar (or lump sugar)
- Club soda

Pour Tequila, lime juice and nectar into a collins glass with ice. Stir thoroughly. Top with club soda and garnish with a lime wedge.

The Paloma

- 2 parts Tequila
- Squeeze of lime juice per cocktail
- Grapefruit soda (like Squirt or Jarritos)

Fill a highball glass with ice. Add Tequila and lime juice, top with grapefruit soda. Garnish with a wedge of lime.

Matador

- 1½ parts Gold Tequila
- 3 parts pineapple juice
- ½ part lime juice

Shake with ice. Strain into an ice filled old fashioned or cocktail glass.

33

SHOT
Cinnamon Whiskey

MIX
Brandy & Soda

COCKTAIL
Juan Collins

| JANUARY 20TH – FEBRUARY 18TH | **Aquarius** *the water bearer* | RULING PLANET URANUS |

This sign is known for their unique perspectives and ability to see the best in humanity. Often accused of being the least emotional of the air signs, Aquarians see the big picture in a way the others in the zodiac do not. Creative, intelligent and cosmic, these 11th house rulers are the humanitarians of the zodiac, known for their contributions to the greater good and their freedom loving nature. The 11th house is known as the house of friendships or social associations. Aquarians are ruled by Uranus, the planet of upheaval and change, they are not afraid of the unknown. *Make sure you pick a spot for drinks with lots of people watching opportunities.*

The Juan Collins is a distinctive take on a classic drink. Perfect for Aquarians.

Juan Collins

- ½ oz. of Tequila
- 1 oz. of lemon juice
- 1 oz. of agave nectar
- club soda
- lime wedge

Pour Tequila, lime juice and nectar into a collins glass with ice cubes. Stir thoroughly. Top with club soda and garnish with lime wedge.

RTH GEM

Alluring Amethyst

Saturday

LUCKY DAY & NUMBER

8 & 1

famous PEOPLE

Farrah Fawcett
John Belushi
John Travolta

Burt Reynolds
Angela Davis
Yoko Ono

Liqueur & Aperitif

Pisco Sour

- 2 parts Pisco
- 1 part fresh lime juice
- 1 lump sugar
- 1 egg white
- 3 dashes Angostura Bitters

Shake Pisco, juice, sugar and egg white vigorously with ice and strain into a cocktail glass. Garnish with a lime slice and 3 drops of Angostura Bitters.

The Adonis

- 1½ parts Dry Sherry
- 1½ parts Sweet Vermouth
- 2 to 3 dashes Orange Bitters

Stir briskly with ice until thoroughly chilled. Strain into the chilled cocktail glass.

Grasshopper

- 1 part Crème de Menthe (green)
- 1 part Crème de Cacao (white)
- 1 part fresh cream

Shake well with ice. Strain into a chilled cocktail glass.

Americano

- 1½ parts Campari
- 1½ parts Sweet Vermouth
- 3 oz. chilled club soda

Fill a chilled rocks glass with ice. Add the Campari, Sweet Vermouth and club soda and stir well. Garnish with an orange wheel and lemon twist.

Pimm's Cup

- 1 part PIMM'S No.1
- 2 parts lemonade
- Mint, orange, strawberries
- English cucumber to garnish
- Ice

Put the ingredients in a tall glass, mix, garnish with thin slice of cucumber. (Increase proportionally for a pitcher of Pimm's Cup).

Aperol Spritz

- 4½ parts Brut Prosecco
- 2½ parts Aperol
- 1 oz. club soda

Pour the Prosecco into a collins glass filled with ice. Add the Aperol and a lime or orange slice, top with club soda.

SHOT
Rum

MIX
Sea Breeze

COCKTAIL
Club Cocktail

| FEBRUARY 19TH – MARCH 20TH | **Pisces**
the fishes | RULING PLANET
NEPTUNE |

Known as the most
intuitive sign of the zodiac,
Pisces are known for their empathetic
understanding of those around them. The
fish is know for their artistic creativity, ability to
befriend people from all walks of life and living life both
above and under the water. Ruled by the 12th house, the
house of the unseen. Whilst traditionally associated with
self-undoing and confinement, the 12th house also talks to
us about working through our subconscious issues and
bringing them to the surface. Pisces are known for their
ability to dig deep into the world beyond the veil and
life beyond the surface. *Ruled by Neptune, the lord
of the sea, here are some imaginative drinks that
are sure to net a favorable result from the
fish in your life.*

This imaginative and gently flavored cocktail is a good catch for Pisces.

Club Cocktail

- 2 oz. Brandy
- ½ oz. Maraschino Liqueur
- ½ oz.. pineapple juice
- 2 dashes Peychaud Bitters

Shake all ingredients well with ice and strain into a martini or cocktail glass. Garnish with a twist of lemon peel and a strawberry, and serve.

BIRTH GEM

The Aquamarine

LUCKY DAY & NUMBER

Friday

8 & 2

famous PEOPLE

George Harrison
Lou Reed
Sly Stone

Johnny Cash
Quincy Jones
Nina Simone

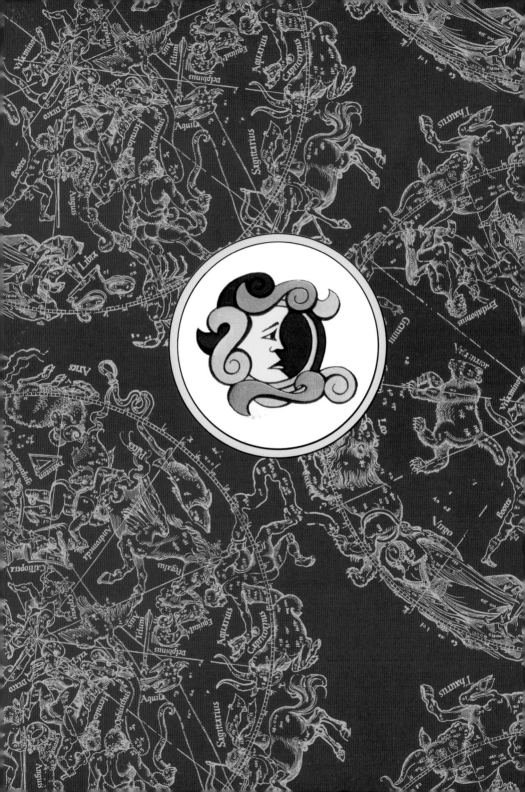